Why Certification Matters

How Working with a Middle Credit Score®
Certified Lender and Realtor Protects Your
Credit, Your Time, and Your Outcome

Copyright Page

Why Certification Matters
How Working with a Middle Credit Score® Certified Lender
and Realtor Protects Your Credit, Your Time, and Your
Outcome

Printed in the United States of America.

ISBN: 979-8-9945570-2-0
First Edition

Dedicated to consumers navigating complex decisions without clear guidance.

Contents

Introduction

This book was written to address a gap that has existed quietly for decades.

Buying or refinancing a home is one of the most consequential financial decisions most consumers will ever make. It involves credit, timing, coordination, and trust. Yet most people move through the process without a clear framework for understanding how credit is evaluated or how professionals should align when credit influences outcomes.

The confusion that consumers experience is rarely the result of negligence or lack of preparation. It is the result of structural separation. Real estate and lending are licensed disciplines with defined responsibilities, yet credit literacy lives between them. It influences nearly every decision, but it has never been formally integrated into a shared interpretive standard.

This book does not attempt to teach consumers how to repair credit, calculate scores, or navigate underwriting guidelines independently. It exists for a different purpose. It explains why alignment between professionals matters, how role clarity protects consumers, and why certification exists to reinforce consistent behavior when decisions become complex.

Middle Credit Score® Certification was created to provide a structured framework for understanding how credit influences timing, communication, and coordination. It does not replace licensing. It does not override professional authority. It reinforces shared expectations across roles so that guidance remains disciplined rather than improvised.

This book is written for multiple audiences. For consumers, it provides clarity about what to look for in the professionals guiding them. For Realtors and lenders, it reinforces role boundaries and coordination standards. For brokerages and institutions, it offers a framework that strengthens professionalism without disrupting existing systems.

Certification is not a title. It is a behavioral standard. It reflects how professionals operate when uncertainty appears, when timing matters, and when restraint protects more than urgency.

Understanding that distinction is the beginning of alignment.

And alignment is what protects outcomes.

Chapter 1
The Consumer Has Been Guessing

For decades, consumers have been asked to make some of the most important financial decisions of their lives without ever being given a framework for understanding who they should trust. Buying a home, applying for a mortgage, and navigating credit are presented as routine milestones, yet the process itself is rarely explained in a way that empowers the consumer. Instead, buyers are expected to rely on confidence, familiarity, or reassurance from professionals they may have just met, often without understanding how differently those professionals approach credit, timing, and risk.

In my career, I have watched this play out thousands of times. Consumers assume that all lenders evaluate credit the same way and that all Realtors share the same level of understanding when it comes to how credit affects approvals, timelines, and options. That assumption feels reasonable, because no one ever tells them otherwise. The system does not offer consumers a way to evaluate guidance before it matters. It does not explain that two professionals can be well intentioned and experienced, yet operate from completely different levels of understanding when credit becomes part of the equation.

When credit enters the picture, the process often begins to feel unpredictable. A consumer may be confident one day and uncertain the next. A conversation that sounded reassuring can suddenly lead to a pause, a delay, or a rejection that no one anticipated. In those moments, consumers often blame themselves. They assume they misunderstood something, waited too long, acted too quickly, or failed to do something they were never told to do in the first place. What they do not realize is that the confusion they are experiencing is not the result of personal failure. It is the result of a system that was never designed to teach consumers how to evaluate guidance or recognize alignment.

Most consumers are never taught the difference between advice and education. Advice tells someone what to do. Education explains why something matters, when it matters, and when it does not. Consumers are also rarely taught to distinguish confidence from competence. A professional can sound certain, speak clearly, and still be operating without a structured understanding of how credit impacts outcomes. Intent is often mistaken for alignment. Good intentions do not always lead to good results, especially in a credit driven process where timing, restraint, and interpretation matter.

Because these distinctions are never explained, guessing becomes the default behavior. Consumers guess which professional to trust. They guess whether guidance is accurate. They guess whether a setback is normal or a warning sign. They guess whether they should move forward or pause. Guessing feels manageable until it is not. When credit becomes the deciding factor, guessing becomes risky. Decisions made without clarity can create delays, unnecessary stress, and avoidable damage to credit that follows consumers far beyond a single transaction.

This book is not written to assign blame or criticize professionals. Many lenders and Realtors work hard, care deeply about their clients, and want to do the right thing. The problem is not effort. The problem is that consumers have never been given a clear way to understand how guidance differs, why roles matter, and what alignment actually looks like in practice. Without that understanding, even well meaning guidance can lead consumers down the wrong path.

The purpose of this book is to replace guessing with clarity. Not by teaching consumers how to analyze credit reports or calculate scores, but by helping them understand what responsible guidance looks like and why certification exists. When consumers understand how to recognize aligned professionals, they stop relying on enthusiasm alone and start valuing structure, education, and restraint. That shift changes outcomes. It also changes trust, not through promises, but through understanding.

Why the System Never Taught Consumers How to Choose

For most consumers, the home buying and mortgage process begins with trust rather than understanding. The system assumes that consumers will rely on professionals to guide them and that those professionals will naturally be aligned. What the system never explains is how differently guidance can be delivered depending on training, role clarity, and approach. Consumers were never taught how to evaluate guidance because the system was not designed for evaluation. It was designed for participation.

In lending and real estate, education has historically focused on transactions, not interpretation. Consumers are taught what steps come next, not why those steps matter or who is responsible for which decisions. This leaves consumers dependent on confidence rather than clarity. When everything goes smoothly, that dependency feels harmless. When credit becomes a factor, it becomes risky.

Confidence Feels Like Competence Until It Is Tested

Most consumers equate confidence with knowledge. A professional who speaks clearly, reassures quickly, and moves the process forward often feels trustworthy. In many cases, that confidence is genuine. The problem arises when confidence is not supported by structured understanding. Credit driven decisions test guidance in ways that surface gaps only when timing tightens or outcomes change.

Competence reveals itself under pressure. It shows up in how explanations are given, how expectations are set, and how restraint is exercised. Consumers rarely see this distinction early because nothing requires it yet. By the time confidence is tested, decisions may already be in motion.

Why Guessing Became the Default

Guessing did not become the default because consumers are careless. It became the default because no alternative was ever presented. Consumers guess which professional to trust. They guess which guidance matters most. They guess whether a delay is normal or a warning sign. They guess whether to act or wait. This guessing feels manageable until it is not.

When consumers lack a framework, they fill the gap with assumptions. Those assumptions are shaped by familiarity, urgency, or reassurance rather than understanding. Certification exists to replace guessing with recognition. It gives consumers a way to understand how guidance differs before consequences appear.

Why This Matters Before Credit Enters the Conversation

By the time credit becomes the focus, the cost of guessing increases. Decisions carry more weight, timing becomes more sensitive, and options narrow. Consumers who understand how to recognize aligned professionals earlier experience fewer surprises later. This chapter is not about teaching credit. It is about teaching awareness. Awareness of how guidance is delivered, how roles differ, and why alignment matters before pressure appears.

Certification exists because consumers deserve clarity before stakes rise. When consumers understand that guidance quality matters more than enthusiasm, they stop guessing and start choosing with intention. That shift changes outcomes and explains why this conversation must begin before credit becomes the breaking point.

Chapter 2
Certification Is Not a Title, It Is a Signal

When consumers hear the word certification, they often assume it is simply another title or credential added to a professional's name. In many industries, certifications are presented as marketing tools, designed to differentiate one professional from another without clearly explaining what that distinction actually means for the person being served. In the context of credit driven decisions, certification must mean something very different. It must signal how a professional thinks, how they communicate, and how they protect the consumer when the process becomes complex.

Middle Credit Score® Certification is not about claiming superiority or suggesting that one professional is better than another. It is about alignment. Certification signals that a lender or Realtor has been trained to understand where their role begins and ends, how credit influences outcomes, and how to guide consumers without crossing boundaries that can cause confusion or harm. This training is not focused on tactics or shortcuts. It is focused on structure, interpretation, and ethical restraint.

There is an important difference between experience and education. Years in the business do not automatically translate into structured understanding. Many professionals gain experience by repeating processes without ever stepping back to understand why those processes work or fail. Certification introduces a shared framework that connects experience to education. It ensures that guidance is not based on assumptions or habits, but on a consistent understanding of how credit, timing, and communication interact. For the consumer, this consistency matters more than charisma, confidence, or tenure.

Certification also establishes ethical boundaries. A certified professional understands what they are responsible for and what they are not. They know when to explain, when to pause, and when to redirect a consumer to the appropriate professional. This restraint is not a limitation. It is a form of protection. When professionals operate within clearly defined roles, consumers receive guidance that is clearer, safer, and more reliable.

Most importantly, certification exists for the consumer, not the professional. It gives consumers a way to filter guidance before consequences appear. It signals that a professional values education over opinion, clarity over reassurance, and long-term outcomes over short term momentum. When consumers begin to recognize certification as a signal of alignment rather than a badge of status, the entire decision making process changes. Trust becomes informed, not assumed, and that shift is where better outcomes begin.

CERTIFICATION IS NOT A TITLE, IT IS A SIGNAL

Why Titles Do Not Tell the Whole Story

Consumers are surrounded by titles. Loan officer, mortgage specialist, Realtor, broker. These titles describe roles, but they do not explain how those roles are performed. Two professionals can hold the same title and approach the process in entirely different ways. One may prioritize explanation and coordination. Another may rely on reassurance and momentum. From the outside, those differences are difficult to see until pressure reveals them.

Certification exists to communicate what a title cannot. It signals how a professional has been trained to think, how they approach responsibility, and how they behave when clarity matters more than speed. This signal is not about status. It is about approach.

What Certification Signals in Real Time

A certification signal appears in moments that matter. It shows up in how expectations are set early rather than corrected later. It appears in how questions are answered without overreach. It becomes visible when a professional pauses instead of reacting and coordinates instead of assuming.

Consumers do not need to understand the curriculum behind certification to benefit from it. They experience the signal through communication style, restraint, and consistency. Over time, these signals become recognizable. They feel different because they are different.

Experience Alone Does Not Create Consistency

Years in business can produce familiarity, but familiarity does not guarantee consistency. Experience teaches what has worked before, but it does not always create a shared framework for how decisions should be guided across roles. Without that framework, guidance varies depending on the individual rather than the process.

Certification introduces structured understanding that experience alone cannot provide. It aligns professionals around how credit is discussed, how boundaries are respected, and how consumers are protected. This alignment creates consistency across conversations, teams, and transactions.

Why Certification Exists for the Consumer

Certification is often misunderstood as something professionals earn for themselves. In this context, certification exists for the consumer. It was created to reduce uncertainty, prevent mixed messaging, and make guidance more predictable. It does not elevate one professional above another. It establishes shared standards for how guidance is delivered.

When consumers recognize certification as a signal rather than a badge, their decision-making changes. They stop evaluating confidence and start evaluating clarity. They listen for explanation rather than reassurance. Certification simplifies choice by making approach visible before consequences appear.

Certification as a Filter, Not a Label

A label identifies. A filter clarifies. Certification functions as a filter by helping consumers recognize alignment without confrontation or comparison. It does not require consumers to test professionals or challenge expertise. It allows them to observe how professionals operate and choose accordingly.

This distinction matters. Certification does not create exclusivity. It creates transparency. It does not promise outcomes. It promotes consistency. By functioning as a filter, certification supports informed choice and reinforces why guidance quality matters more than enthusiasm.

Chapter 3:
Why Alignment Matters More Than Expertise

Experience has long been treated as the primary measure of professional competence. Years in business, volume of transactions, and familiarity with the process are often assumed to be enough. While experience has value, it does not guarantee alignment. In a credit driven environment, expertise without alignment can create just as many problems as inexperience. What matters most is not how much a professional knows in isolation, but how that knowledge is applied within a clearly defined role.

Alignment refers to how professionals operate within the system; not how impressive their background appears. An aligned professional understands where their responsibility begins and ends. They communicate within those boundaries, coordinate with other professionals rather than override them, and recognize when restraint is more protective than action. Expertise can inform decisions, but alignment governs behavior. Without alignment, even well-informed professionals can create confusion, mixed messaging, and unintended consequences.

Consumers rarely experience misalignment as a technical problem. They experience it as uncertainty. Guidance sounds confident, yet outcomes change. Conversations feel reassuring, yet expectations shift. In many cases, the issue is not that someone lacked knowledge. It is that multiple professionals operated from different assumptions, offered guidance from overlapping roles, or moved forward without confirming shared understanding. Alignment prevents these breakdowns by ensuring that expertise is applied consistently and responsibly.

Certification exists to reinforce alignment, not to elevate status. It provides a shared framework that helps professionals recognize how their actions affect the broader process. When professionals are aligned, communication becomes clearer, coordination improves, and consumers receive guidance that feels steady rather than reactive. Alignment reduces the need for correction because it minimizes the conditions that create confusion in the first place.

In a complex system, expertise alone does not protect consumers. Alignment does. It ensures that experience is translated into clarity, that confidence is supported by structure, and that guidance is delivered with discipline. As processes accelerate and decisions become more compressed, alignment becomes the differentiator that holds outcomes together. This is why alignment matters more than expertise, and why certification is designed to reinforce behavior, not hierarchy.

Expertise Solves Problems. Alignment Prevents Them.

Expertise is often reactive by nature. It is developed through experience with past situations and applied when something needs to be fixed, explained, or corrected. Alignment works earlier. It shapes how professionals think before problems arise and how they behave before decisions are made. In a system influenced by credit, timing, and coordination, prevention matters more than recovery.

When professionals are aligned, fewer problems require expertise to resolve. Expectations are set earlier. Roles are respected. Conversations are sequenced intentionally. Expertise still matters, but it is applied within a framework that reduces the likelihood of confusion. Alignment does not replace knowledge. It governs how knowledge is used.

Why Consumers Feel the Effects of Misalignment First

Consumers are usually the first to experience misalignment, even if they cannot identify it. They hear confident guidance that later changes. They receive reassurance that does not match outcomes. They are told that something is normal without understanding why it happened. These experiences create doubt, not because

the professionals lacked knowledge, but because that
knowledge was not coordinated.

Misalignment places the burden of interpretation on the
consumer. They are left to decide which guidance
matters, whose advice to follow, and when to act.
Alignment removes that burden by ensuring that
professionals operate from shared assumptions and
communicate with consistency. When alignment is
present, consumers feel steadiness rather than surprise.

Why Alignment Is a Behavioral Standard, Not a Skill

Skills can be learned and applied selectively. Alignment is
a standard that shapes behavior across situations. It
influences how professionals respond under pressure,
how they communicate uncertainty, and how they handle
moments when restraint is more appropriate than action.
Alignment does not depend on personality or style. It
depends on shared understanding.

Certification reinforces alignment by creating common
expectations for behavior. It does not dictate decisions. It
clarifies responsibility. Professionals who are aligned do
not compete for authority or override one another. They
coordinate. This coordination protects the process and
preserves trust when outcomes are still unfolding.

Experience Without Alignment Creates Variability

Two professionals with similar experience can produce very different consumer experiences. One may communicate clearly, pause appropriately, and coordinate early. Another may rely on momentum, reassurance, or assumption. The difference is not intelligence or intent. It is alignment.

Experience accumulates individually. Alignment is shared. Without alignment, experience produces variability. With alignment, experience becomes an asset that supports consistency. Certification exists to reduce this variability so that consumers receive predictable guidance regardless of who they work with or where they are located.

Why Alignment Scales When Expertise Alone Does Not

Expertise scales through individuals. Alignment scales through systems. As real estate and lending become more interconnected and more automated, reliance on individual expertise becomes less reliable. Systems move faster than any one person can react. Alignment provides stability because it creates shared behavior across professionals and roles.

Certification supports this scalability by reinforcing principles that hold regardless of market conditions or transaction type. It ensures that guidance remains consistent even as processes evolve. This is why alignment matters more than expertise. It is not a judgment of knowledge. It is a recognition of what protects outcomes when complexity increases.

Chapter 4:
What a Middle Credit Score® Certified Lender Knows

A Middle Credit Score® Certified Lender approaches the mortgage process differently long before an application is submitted. Their value is not rooted in optimism or reassurance. It is rooted in understanding how mortgage credit is evaluated in the real world and how small decisions can influence outcomes in ways most consumers never see. Certified lenders do not treat credit as a number to overcome. They treat it as a system that must be interpreted carefully and respected throughout the process.

Certified lenders understand why the middle credit score matters and how it becomes the reference point for most mortgage decisions. More importantly, they understand how timing interacts with credit. They know when actions are likely to help, when they are likely to have no effect, and when they can unintentionally cause harm. This awareness allows them to plan rather than react. It also allows them to protect consumers from taking steps that feel productive but create delays, additional scrutiny, or outright denials later in the process.

One of the most important skills a certified lender brings to the table is the ability to explain outcomes clearly. When a result changes or a challenge appears, certified lenders can explain why it happened, what factors are actually influencing the decision, and what matters next. Just as important, they can explain what does not matter. This clarity reduces anxiety and prevents consumers from making unnecessary moves based on fear or misinformation. Explanation replaces guessing, and planning replaces hope.

Certified lenders are also trained to communicate clarity without making promises. They understand that certainty in lending is often misunderstood and that false reassurance can be more damaging than honest restraint. Rather than promising approval or timelines, certified lenders focus on preparing consumers for what is realistic, what is controllable, and what requires patience. This approach stabilizes the process and helps consumers stay grounded when pressure increases.

By the end of a transaction, most consumers realize that the greatest value a certified lender provided was not access to a product, but interpretation and protection. Certified lenders act as educators and interpreters during moments of uncertainty. They remain steady when outcomes shift, and they prioritize long term consumer well being over short term momentum. That calm competence is what separates certified lenders from those who rely on confidence alone, and it is why certification matters when credit is involved.

Chapter 5:
What a Middle Credit Score® Certified Realtor Knows

A Middle Credit Score® Certified Realtor understands that credit influences nearly every part of a real estate transaction, even when it is not openly discussed. While Realtors do not interpret credit or determine qualification, certified Realtors understand how credit impacts timing, affordability, and overall strategy. This awareness allows them to guide consumers through the process with greater care, reducing the risk of rushed decisions or misplaced confidence.

Certified Realtors know when it is appropriate to move forward and when it is wiser to pause. They recognize early signals that a lender should be brought into the conversation sooner rather than later, not to slow momentum, but to protect it. By coordinating effectively with certified lenders, they help ensure that expectations are aligned before pressure increases. This coordination often prevents surprises that can derail transactions later in the process.

One of the most valuable qualities of a certified Realtor is their understanding of role boundaries. Certified Realtors do not offer credit advice or attempt to interpret financial information. Instead, they focus on managing the process itself. They protect consumers from misinformation by redirecting questions to the appropriate professional and from overconfidence by reinforcing the importance of preparation. This restraint is not hesitation. It is intentional protection.

Certified Realtors also act as advocates for clarity. They help consumers understand where decisions fit within the broader transaction and when additional guidance is needed. By resisting the urge to provide answers outside their role, certified Realtors reduce risk and create a more stable experience for everyone involved. Their value lies not in telling consumers what to do with credit, but in knowing when to slow the process, bring the right professionals together, and keep the transaction aligned. That discipline is what protects the consumer and keeps outcomes on track.

Process Awareness Is Not the Same as Credit Interpretation

A certified Realtor understands how credit influences the real estate process without attempting to interpret credit itself. This distinction matters. Credit affects timing, affordability, and strategy, but interpreting credit belongs to the lender. A certified Realtor recognizes where credit fits into the process and how it can shape decisions without stepping into analysis or advice.

This awareness allows certified Realtors to coordinate intelligently. They know when credit considerations should influence next steps and when to pause rather than push forward. By respecting this boundary, they protect consumers from confusion and prevent guidance from becoming fragmented.

Knowing When to Move Forward Is as Important as Knowing When to Pause

Momentum feels productive, especially in competitive markets. However, movement without alignment can create risk. Certified Realtors are trained to recognize moments when moving forward is appropriate and moments when waiting protects the consumer. This judgment is not about hesitation. It is about timing.

Certified Realtors understand that a pause can preserve options, prevent missteps, and allow for clearer planning. They do not interpret the pause as a setback. They see it as a strategic decision that supports long term outcomes rather than short term progress.

Early Coordination Prevents Late Corrections

One of the most valuable skills a certified Realtor develops is knowing when to involve a lender earlier than expected. Early coordination allows conversations to happen before assumptions solidify. It reduces the need for corrections later in the process, when changes feel disruptive or stressful.

Certified Realtors do not wait for problems to appear before bringing professionals together. They understand that alignment established early protects everyone involved. This approach creates smoother transactions and reduces the likelihood that consumers will be surprised by information they assumed had already been considered.

Protecting Consumers From Overconfidence and Misinformation

Consumers often receive advice from many sources, some well intended and others uninformed. Certified Realtors act as process guardians by helping consumers slow down and redirect questions to the appropriate professional. They protect consumers from acting on misinformation and from overconfidence that can lead to rushed decisions.

This protection does not involve correction or confrontation. It involves clarity. Certified Realtors know how to guide conversations back to alignment without undermining trust. By doing so, they preserve the integrity of the process and reinforce confidence rooted in understanding rather than assumption.

Why Boundaries Increase a Realtor's Value

Some consumers assume that more advice equals more value. In reality, value often comes from knowing what not to provide. Certified Realtors increase their value by staying within their role and coordinating effectively with lenders. This discipline reduces risk and strengthens trust.

When Realtors respect boundaries, consumers experience fewer mixed messages and greater clarity. The Realtor becomes a steady presence rather than another voice to reconcile. This role clarity is not a limitation. It is a professional advantage that protects outcomes and reinforces why certification matters.

Chapter 6:
What Realtors Do Not Do (And Why That Protects You)

One of the most important protections a consumer can have in a real estate transaction is working with a Realtor who understands what not to do. In a credit driven process, restraint is not a weakness. It is a safeguard. Middle Credit Score® Certified Realtors are trained to recognize that their role is not to interpret credit, evaluate qualification, or recommend financial actions. These limits exist for a reason, and when respected, they protect everyone involved.

Realtors are often the first professionals consumers interact with, and that position creates trust. When questions about credit arise, it can feel natural for a realtor to want to help by offering suggestions or opinions. However, guidance that extends beyond coordination and into credit interpretation can create confusion, conflicting information, and unintended consequences. Certified Realtors understand that even well-meaning advice can cause harm when it is offered without full context or proper timing.

Avoiding credit advice reduces risk in several ways. It prevents consumers from acting on incomplete or inaccurate information. It reduces the chance of unnecessary credit activity that can impact outcomes later. It also ensures that responsibility remains clearly defined, so consumers receive explanations from the professionals trained to provide them. When Realtors stay within their role, consumers are less likely to receive mixed messages or feel pressure to make decisions they do not fully understand.

Certification reinforces this discipline by teaching Realtors how to recognize when to pause, when to coordinate, and when to redirect. Rather than trying to solve every problem themselves, certified Realtors focus on protecting the process. They create space for the right conversations to happen at the right time, involving the appropriate professionals. This approach improves outcomes not by adding steps, but by preventing missteps.

For consumers, a realtor who does not give credit advice is often the safest one. It signals professionalism, respect for boundaries, and a commitment to clarity. Certification teaches that knowing what not to do is just as important as knowing what to do. That understanding builds trust, reassures consumers, and strengthens collaboration with lenders. It also explains why certification exists in the first place: to ensure that guidance is responsible, aligned, and protective rather than reactive.

———————————————

Chapter 7:
When Credit Becomes the Breaking Point

For most consumers, credit does not feel stressful at the beginning of a transaction. Early conversations are often optimistic, timelines feel manageable, and expectations are based on assumptions that have not yet been tested. The pressure does not usually appear right away. It emerges when credit intersects with deadlines, contract terms, or decisions that can no longer be postponed. That is the moment when credit stops being abstract and becomes personal.

Most deals do not fall apart early. They falter when assumptions meet reality and when expectations were never clearly set. Timelines tighten, new information surfaces, and conversations change tone. Consumers often experience this shift as confusion or embarrassment, followed by panic when outcomes no longer feel predictable. In these moments, people look for quick answers, even when the situation requires careful interpretation and restraint. For many consumers, this moment passes without ever being clearly identified, yet it quietly reshapes the entire transaction from that point forward.

Certified professionals recognize this pressure point long before it arrives. They understand that credit rarely creates problems on its own. Surprises do. When consumers are not prepared for how credit will be evaluated or when key conversations happen too late, the process becomes reactive. Uncertified processes respond to stress as it appears, often adjusting on the fly. Certified professionals plan for these moments in advance, reducing the likelihood that a single development will derail the entire transaction.

Preparation does not eliminate challenges, but it changes how they are handled. When expectations are aligned early and roles are respected, consumers are less likely to feel blindsided. Certified professionals provide stability during moments of uncertainty by explaining what is happening, what matters, and what can wait. That steadiness prevents emotional decisions and preserves momentum.

By the end of this chapter, it becomes clear that credit itself is rarely the breaking point. The breaking point is uncertainty. Certification exists to replace reaction with anticipation, and chaos with structure. When professionals plan for pressure instead of responding to it, outcomes hold together even when the process becomes difficult.

Chapter 8:
Why Some Deals Stall (And Others Don't)

Most stalled transactions do not fail because someone did not try hard enough. They stall because the process became misaligned. Information was incomplete, roles began to overlap, or assumptions went unchallenged long enough to create friction. When this happens, even motivated consumers and dedicated professionals can find themselves stuck, waiting for clarity that should have existed earlier.

Misalignment often shows up in subtle ways. A Realtor may move forward with confidence before all conversations have taken place. A lender may be brought into the process later than ideal, after expectations have already been set. A consumer may misunderstand timelines or believe that progress means certainty. None of these situations involve bad intent. They involve gaps in coordination. When those gaps widen, the process slows, resets occur, and momentum is lost.

Certified teams move differently because they operate from a shared understanding. Coordination happens earlier. Communication is clearer and more consistent. Conversations are sequenced intentionally rather than reactively. Certified professionals do not assume alignment. They confirm it. This approach reduces the need for resets and minimizes the confusion that often causes transactions to stall midway through the process.

Effort alone does not keep a deal moving. Alignment does. When each professional understands their role and respects the boundaries of others, the process becomes more stable. Certification supports this stability by providing a common framework that keeps everyone in sync. Over time, consumers begin to recognize that successful outcomes are rarely the result of one individual. They are the result of coordinated teams operating with clarity. That understanding changes how trust is formed and why certification matters when progress feels uncertain.

Stalled Deals Are Rarely About One Thing

Most stalled transactions are not the result of a single mistake. They are the result of small misalignments compounding over time. A conversation that happened too late. A role that blurred slightly. An assumption that was never challenged because everyone believed things were moving in the right direction.

From the consumer's perspective, a stalled deal feels sudden. Progress was happening, expectations were set, and then momentum slowed or stopped. What consumers rarely see is that the stall usually began much earlier, long before any visible issue appeared. Certified professionals understand that stalls are not events. They are outcomes.

Effort Does Not Replace Alignment

When a deal begins to stall, the natural reaction is to work harder. More calls. More emails. More reassurance. While effort feels productive, it does not correct misalignment. In some cases, increased effort adds pressure without adding clarity.

Alignment determines whether effort helps or hurts. When professionals are aligned, effort reinforces progress. When they are not, effort amplifies confusion. Certified professionals recognize that slowing down to realign roles and expectations often restores momentum more effectively than pushing forward blindly.

Where Most Stalls Actually Begin

Many stalls originate in the early stages of a transaction, when enthusiasm is high and caution feels unnecessary. A Realtor moves forward assuming credit is stable. A lender is brought in after key decisions have already been framed. A consumer believes timelines are firm because no one explained what could affect them.

None of these moments feel risky in isolation. Together, they create conditions where a stall becomes likely. Certified professionals focus on these early moments because that is where alignment is easiest to establish and most effective.

Certified Teams Move Differently

Certified teams coordinate earlier, communicate more intentionally, and challenge assumptions before they harden into expectations. This does not mean they eliminate uncertainty. It means they acknowledge it honestly. When uncertainty is named early, it becomes manageable. When it appears late, it feels disruptive.

Consumers working with certified professionals often notice fewer resets and less backtracking. Not because the process is simpler, but because alignment reduces the need to undo decisions made without full context. This difference is subtle but powerful.

Why Stalls Feel Personal to Consumers

When a deal stalls, consumers often internalize it. They wonder what they did wrong or what they failed to understand. This reaction is natural, but it is rarely accurate. Stalls are almost always systemic, not personal. They reflect how information, timing, and guidance interacted, not the consumer's worth or readiness.

Certified professionals are trained to normalize stalls without minimizing them. They explain what is happening, why it matters, and what comes next. This clarity preserves trust and keeps consumers grounded while alignment is restored.

Alignment Keeps Deals Moving, Even When They Pause

A pause does not equal a stall. Pauses can be intentional, protective, and productive. Stalls happen when pauses are unplanned and unexplained. Certified professionals distinguish between the two.

When alignment is present, even a pause feels controlled. Consumers understand why it is happening and what it protects. That understanding allows the process to move forward with confidence rather than frustration. This is why alignment, not urgency, determines whether deals hold together or quietly fall apart.

What This Chapter Is Really Teaching

This chapter is not about blame, mistakes, or correction. It is about recognition. Recognition that stalled deals are often preventable. Recognition that alignment matters more than effort. Recognition that professionals who operate from shared understanding protect momentum without pressure.

Certified professionals do not promise smooth transactions. They provide structured guidance that keeps uncertainty from turning into delay. That distinction explains why some deals stall and others do not.

Chapter 9:
The Cost of Mixed Messages

Mixed messages rarely come from bad intent. They come from multiple professionals operating without alignment, each offering guidance from their own perspective, often without realizing how those messages intersect. To a consumer, those messages blur together. What begins as reassurance can quickly become confusion, and confusion creates hesitation, stress, and poor decision making.

In a real estate or lending process, consumers often hear different versions of the truth depending on who they speak with and when. A Realtor may express confidence based on progress. A lender may raise caution based on timing. A well-meaning third party may offer advice without understanding the full picture. None of these messages are necessarily wrong on their own. The problem arises when they are delivered without coordination. When guidance is not aligned, consumers are left to reconcile contradictions they were never equipped to interpret.

The cost of mixed messages is not always immediate, but it is always real. Consumers begin to question which guidance matters most. They hesitate, overcorrect, or act prematurely. Momentum is lost, expectations shift, and trust erodes. In many stalled or failed transactions, the root cause is not credit, pricing, or qualification. It is the accumulation of conflicting signals that forced the consumer to guess which voice to follow.

Certified professionals are trained to reduce mixed messaging by respecting role clarity and sequencing communication intentionally. They understand that timing matters as much as content. A message delivered too early, too late, or without context can create more harm than silence. Certification reinforces the importance of coordination so that consumers hear consistent guidance, even when the message itself is cautious or incomplete.

Alignment does not require agreement on every detail. It requires shared understanding of roles and responsibility. When professionals are aligned, they communicate in a way that supports clarity rather than competition. They avoid overriding one another, correcting publicly, or creating urgency without explanation. This discipline protects consumers from the burden of interpretation and allows decisions to unfold with confidence rather than pressure.

Mixed messages place the weight of the process on the consumer. Alignment removes that burden. Certification exists to ensure that guidance feels coherent, deliberate, and trustworthy. When consumers receive consistent signals, they are able to move forward with understanding rather than confusion. That clarity protects outcomes and explains why alignment is not optional when credit, timing, and guidance intersect.

Mixed Messages Do Not Sound Confusing at First

Mixed messages rarely announce themselves as a problem. They usually sound reasonable in isolation. One person says one thing. Another adds context. A third offers reassurance. None of it feels wrong at the moment.

The confusion appears later, when those messages collide. Consumers are left trying to reconcile guidance that was never designed to work together. What sounded helpful early becomes destabilizing when decisions must be made.

Certified professionals understand that clarity is not about giving more information. It is about ensuring information aligns.

Why Consumers Try to Combine Advice That Was Never Meant to Be Combined

Consumers assume that professionals are operating from the same understanding. They believe advice fits together because it comes from credible sources. When it does not, consumers try to make it fit anyway.

This is not a failure of judgment. It is a natural response to authority. When professionals are not aligned, consumers shoulder the burden of interpretation. They attempt to reconcile guidance they were never meant to evaluate. That burden creates stress, hesitation, and second-guessing.

Certification exists to remove that burden.

Good Intentions Still Produce Bad Outcomes

Most mixed messages are delivered with good intent. A Realtor wants to be supportive. A lender wants to be encouraging. Someone offers advice based on past experience. None of this is malicious.

But intent does not equal alignment. When guidance is not coordinated, even well-meaning advice can send consumers in conflicting directions. The outcome is confusion, not clarity. Certified professionals recognize that protecting outcomes requires discipline, not just care.

The Emotional Toll of Conflicting Guidance

When consumers receive mixed messages, they often assume the problem is theirs. They believe they misunderstood something or failed to ask the right question. Confidence erodes quietly. Trust becomes conditional.

This emotional toll rarely shows up in timelines or documents, but it affects every decision that follows. Certified professionals understand that emotional clarity matters. They reduce mixed messages so consumers are not left managing uncertainty they did not create.

Why Fewer Voices Create Better Outcomes

More advice does not equal better guidance. In fact, fewer voices often produce stronger outcomes. Certified professionals coordinate communication intentionally. They know when to speak, when to defer, and when to redirect questions to the appropriate role.

This restraint is not silence. It is structure. When guidance flows through the right channels, consumers experience steadiness rather than contradiction. That steadiness builds confidence even when decisions are complex.

Mixed Messages Create Delay Without Looking Like Delay

One of the most damaging aspects of mixed messages is that they create delay without appearing to. Consumers pause. They hesitate. They seek clarification. Momentum slows quietly.

Certified professionals understand that confusion costs time even when nothing appears wrong on paper. By reducing mixed messages early, they protect progress without adding pressure. Alignment keeps movement intentional.

Why Certification Reduces Noise, Not Choice

Certification does not limit options. It reduces noise. Consumers still have decisions to make. What changes is how clearly those decisions are framed.

Certified professionals do not compete to be the loudest voice. They operate within defined roles so guidance reinforces rather than contradicts. This consistency allows consumers to move forward confidently instead of managing internal conflict.

What This Chapter Is Really Saying

This chapter is not about mistakes. It is about structure. Mixed messages are a symptom of misalignment, not incompetence. Certification addresses the structure, not the people.

When consumers experience a process where guidance feels consistent and intentional, they rarely think about why. When they experience mixed messages, they feel the cost immediately. Certification exists to make clarity the default rather than the exception.

Chapter 10:
The Difference Between Help and Harm

In moments of uncertainty, most people want to help. When credit becomes part of a real estate or lending decision, that instinct often intensifies. Advice is offered quickly, suggestions are shared informally, and reassurance replaces explanation. The intention is almost always positive. The impact, however, is not always helpful. When guidance is incomplete, offered without context, or delivered outside of a defined role, it can unintentionally create harm.

Well intended missteps are common because credit feels approachable on the surface. Telling someone to dispute an item, delay a decision, or take a specific action can sound reasonable when the broader impact is not fully understood. Timing, sequence, and context matter far more than most people realize. A suggestion that might seem harmless in isolation can introduce delays, additional scrutiny, or confusion later in the process. These outcomes rarely come from bad advice. They come from advice given without full awareness of consequences.

Certification trains professionals to recognize when action is appropriate and when restraint is the better choice. Certified professionals learn to pause rather than react, to redirect questions to the appropriate role, and to avoid acting on partial information. This discipline protects consumers from unnecessary moves made under pressure. It also protects the process from becoming fragmented by conflicting guidance.

The safest guidance is often less, not more. Education provides clarity, while unchecked advice can create momentum in the wrong direction. Certified professionals are outcome focused. They understand that saying less at the right moment can preserve time, protect credit, and keep decisions grounded. Over time, consumers begin to trust this restraint. They recognize that discipline, caution, and judgment are not signs of hesitation. They are signs of professionalism, and they are why certification matters when decisions feel urgent.

Chapter 11:
Why Certification Protects Time

Time is one of the most underestimated costs in real estate and lending. Consumers often focus on price, approval, or timing in broad terms, but they rarely anticipate how easily time can be lost through miscommunication, resets, or last minute surprises. When time is wasted, stress increases, options narrow, and decisions feel rushed. In many cases, the loss of time has nothing to do with the consumer and everything to do with how the process was guided.

Delays often come from moments that seem small at first. A credit pull that needs to be repeated. A conversation that should have happened earlier. Information that was assumed rather than confirmed. These setbacks compound quickly. Each reset adds pressure, changes expectations, and forces consumers to adjust plans they believed were already settled. Certified professionals work differently because they understand where these delays originate and how to prevent them before they occur.

Certification emphasizes early clarity and intentional sequencing. Certified professionals ask the right questions sooner, coordinate conversations earlier, and avoid assumption driven steps that create rework later. They do not move the process forward simply to maintain momentum. They move it forward when the foundation is stable. This approach reduces unnecessary repetition and protects consumers from feeling rushed into decisions that should have been planned.

Protecting time does not mean rushing the process. Speed without preparation often creates setbacks that cost more time than they save. Certification prioritizes planning over pressure. When expectations are set clearly and roles are aligned early, the process becomes more predictable. Consumers spend less time reacting to surprises and more time making informed decisions.

Time protection is ultimately a form of respect. It reflects a commitment to guiding consumers thoughtfully rather than pushing them forward prematurely. Certified professionals understand that every delay has a human cost, whether it is added stress, lost opportunity, or uncertainty about what comes next. By planning carefully and coordinating effectively, certification protects time in a way that benefits both the consumer and the outcome.

Time Is the Cost No One Budgets For

Most consumers prepare financially for a real estate transaction. They plan for down payments, closing costs, inspections, and moving expenses. What they do not plan for is time loss. Time lost to rework. Time lost to resets. Time lost to waiting on answers that should have been clarified earlier.

Time becomes expensive when it is wasted. A delayed transaction can affect rate locks, housing plans, job timelines, family logistics, and emotional energy. When time is mishandled, the consumer pays for it in stress long before they ever see it on paper.

Certified professionals understand that time is not neutral. It either supports momentum or erodes it.

Most Delays Are Created, Not Caused

Delays are often blamed on external factors. Appraisals. Underwriting. Market conditions. While these factors exist, many of the most damaging delays are self-inflicted. They come from steps taken out of sequence, conversations that happened too late, or assumptions that were never verified.

A credit pull that should have waited. A contract written before coordination occurred. A decision made before the full picture was understood. Each of these moments adds friction later. Certified professionals are trained to recognize where delay is likely to be created and adjust the sequence before it happens.

Time protection begins with anticipation, not acceleration.

Speed Without Clarity Creates Rework

Consumers are often told that speed is an advantage. Faster offers. Faster approvals. Faster closings. What they are rarely told is that speed without clarity creates rework. Rework costs time. It forces resets, explanations, and revisions that could have been avoided.

Certified professionals do not confuse movement with progress. They understand that the fastest path forward is often the one that pauses briefly to ensure alignment. When clarity comes first, fewer steps need to be undone later. That restraint protects time in a way urgency never can.

Why Certified Professionals Ask Questions Earlier

One of the clearest differences consumers notice when working with certified professionals is timing. Certified professionals ask questions earlier. Not because they want to slow things down, but because they want to prevent surprises from appearing at the worst possible moment.

Early questions create early alignment. They surface issues while options are still flexible. They allow conversations to happen before commitments harden into expectations. This approach may feel slower at the beginning, but it almost always saves time overall. Consumers benefit because fewer decisions need to be revisited under pressure.

Time Loss Is Emotional, Not Just Logistical

When time is wasted, consumers do not experience it as a scheduling issue. They experience it emotionally. Frustration builds. Confidence erodes. Trust weakens. Each delay introduces doubt about whether the process is being handled competently.

Certified professionals recognize the emotional cost of time loss. They communicate intentionally, set expectations clearly, and explain pauses before they occur. This transparency helps consumers remain grounded even when timelines shift. Time feels protected when it is respected.

Why Fewer Resets Matter More Than Faster Closings

Consumers often focus on closing dates. Certified professionals focus on resets. A reset is any moment where progress must be undone or repeated. Re-pulls. Re-approvals. Re-explanations. Re-negotiations. Each reset consumes time and confidence.

Certification reduces resets by emphasizing alignment, sequencing, and role clarity. Fewer resets mean fewer surprises. Fewer surprises mean steadier progress. That steadiness is what consumers remember long after the transaction is complete.

Time Protection Is a Form of Consumer Advocacy

Protecting time is not about efficiency metrics or performance claims. It is about advocacy. Certified professionals advocate for consumers by refusing to waste their time. They do not rush decisions for momentum's sake. They do not allow enthusiasm to override preparation.

When time is protected, consumers feel respected. They feel guided rather than pushed. That experience is often the difference between a transaction that feels chaotic and one that feels controlled, even when challenges appear.

What This Chapter Is Really Saying

This chapter is not about moving faster. It is about moving intentionally. Certification protects time by reducing guesswork, preventing unnecessary repetition, and keeping decisions aligned with reality. That protection shows up quietly, but it is felt deeply.

When consumers look back on a transaction and say it felt smooth, they are usually describing time that was handled well. Certification exists to make that outcome more likely, not by speeding the process up, but by preventing it from breaking down.

Chapter 12:
Why Certification Protects Credit

Credit damage rarely happens because a consumer makes a reckless decision. More often, it happens unintentionally, during moments when pressure is high and clarity is low. A transaction moves forward, timelines tighten, and small actions are taken without fully understanding their impact. By the time the effect shows up, the opportunity to prevent it has already passed.

Unnecessary inquiries, poorly timed actions, and misinterpreted guidance are among the most common risks consumers face during a real estate or lending process. These risks are rarely obvious in the moment. They often appear reasonable, even responsible, when viewed without full context. A suggestion meant to help can lead to unintended consequences when timing, sequence, or responsibility is misunderstood.

Certified professionals approach credit with caution and foresight. They understand when credit related actions matter, when they have little effect, and when the safest choice is to pause entirely. This awareness allows them to guide consumers away from unnecessary activity and toward decisions that preserve flexibility. Certification emphasizes preservation rather than manipulation. The goal is not to move numbers, but to protect options.

During a transaction, credit is especially fragile. Actions that might seem harmless outside of that window can carry greater weight when decisions are actively being evaluated. Certified professionals recognize this sensitivity. They communicate clearly about risk without creating fear, and they prioritize long term outcomes over short term momentum. This restraint helps consumers avoid decisions that feel productive in the moment but compromise stability later.

Protection of credit is ultimately about respect for the consumer's future. Certified professionals understand that credit does not exist only for one transaction. It follows the consumer beyond a single purchase or refinance, influencing opportunities long after the process is complete. By handling credit with care, clarity, and ethical judgment, certification builds trust and reinforces why aligned guidance matters most when the stakes are highest.

Credit Is Most Vulnerable When People Are Trying to Be Helpful

Credit damage rarely happens because someone is careless. It usually happens when someone is trying to help without understanding timing, impact, or consequence. A suggestion made with confidence can create harm if it is not grounded in context. During a real estate transaction, even small actions can carry outsized effects.

Certified professionals understand that credit is not static during a transaction. It is sensitive. It reacts to movement, inquiry, and timing. This is why protection matters more than intervention. Credit does not need to be fixed in the middle of a deal. It needs to be preserved.

Why Timing Matters More Than Tactics

Consumers are often exposed to tactics. Disputes. Paydowns. Account changes. What they are rarely taught is when those actions matter and when they should be avoided entirely. Timing determines whether an action helps, delays, or quietly undermines an outcome.

Certified professionals focus on timing first. They recognize moments when credit activity should pause, moments when information should be clarified, and moments when doing nothing is the safest move. This restraint prevents well-intended actions from creating unintended consequences.

Unnecessary Movement Creates Unnecessary Risk

Credit is often damaged not by major decisions, but by unnecessary movement. Extra inquiries. Premature applications. Advice followed out of urgency rather than understanding. Each movement introduces risk without always adding value.

Certified professionals reduce unnecessary movement by coordinating roles and communication. They do not create urgency around credit activity. They create clarity around what matters and what does not. That clarity protects the consumer from acting out of fear or confusion.

Why Certified Professionals Emphasize Preservation Over Improvement

Improving credit is a long-term process. Transactions are short-term environments. Mixing the two without alignment creates risk. Certified professionals understand that the goal during a transaction is not optimization. It is stability.

Preservation means maintaining what already exists. It means avoiding changes that introduce volatility. Certified professionals frame credit as something to be handled carefully, not manipulated aggressively. This approach protects outcomes and prevents regret after the transaction is complete.

Credit Damage Is Often Invisible Until It Is Too Late

One of the most dangerous aspects of credit damage is that it is rarely immediate. A decision made today may not show impact until weeks later, when options are limited and pressure is high. Consumers are often unaware that an action caused harm until they feel the consequence. Certified professionals work to prevent invisible damage by explaining risk before it materializes. They help consumers understand that silence and patience are sometimes the most protective choices. This foresight separates certified guidance from casual advice.

Why Fewer Voices Protect Credit Better Than More Advice

Consumers often receive credit advice from many directions. Friends. Family. Online forums. Professionals outside the transaction. Each voice may mean well, but mixed guidance increases risk. Conflicting advice encourages action without alignment.

Certified professionals act as stabilizers. They reduce noise rather than add to it. By keeping guidance coordinated and role-appropriate, they help consumers avoid acting on incomplete or contradictory information. Fewer voices create safer outcomes.

Credit Protection Is Long-Term Consumer Advocacy

Protecting credit is not just about closing a transaction. It is about safeguarding the consumer's future options. A decision made under pressure can affect borrowing power long after the transaction ends.

Certified professionals approach credit with long-term awareness. They recognize that protecting credit today preserves opportunity tomorrow. This mindset reinforces trust and positions certification as consumer advocacy rather than transactional convenience.

What This Chapter Is Really Saying

This chapter is not about how to change credit. It is about how to respect it. Certification protects credit by teaching restraint, timing, and coordination. It replaces urgency with understanding and action with intention.

When consumers complete a transaction without unnecessary credit damage, they may never realize what was avoided. That is the point. Protection often goes unnoticed. But it is deeply felt when it is missing.

Chapter 13:

Professional Standards, Public Accountability, and Certification Integrity

Certification carries weight only when it is protected by structure. A credential without accountability becomes decoration. A standard without renewal becomes outdated. Middle Credit Score® Certification was designed to function as a living professional framework, not a one-time designation. For that reason, certification includes ongoing responsibility, public verification, and an ethical commitment that reinforces trust beyond a single transaction.

Professional standards must remain neutral to remain credible. Certification does not promote a company, a platform, or a product. It establishes how professionals operate within defined roles when credit influences outcomes. That distinction is essential. When a standard becomes commercially entangled, its authority weakens. When it remains independent, its credibility strengthens over time. Certification integrity depends on this separation.

Annual renewal is a structural safeguard. Credit interpretation, communication standards, and coordination practices must remain current as markets evolve. Renewal reinforces continued alignment with the framework and confirms that certified professionals remain committed to its principles. It is not designed as a barrier. It is designed as reinforcement. Ongoing participation signals that certification reflects active engagement rather than past completion.

Public verification provides transparency. Each certified professional receives a credential that includes a QR-based verification pathway, allowing consumers, brokerages, and institutions to confirm certification status directly through MiddleCreditScore.com. This public registry does not rank professionals, promote transactions, or influence selection. Its purpose is verification. Transparency strengthens trust because it removes ambiguity. A certification that can be confirmed publicly carries more weight than one that relies on claim alone.

Ethics commitment forms the foundation beneath renewal and verification. Certified professionals affirm adherence to clearly defined boundaries: respecting role clarity, avoiding unauthorized credit interpretation, prioritizing coordination over assumption, and protecting consumer understanding above momentum. This commitment is not symbolic. It reinforces behavior. Certification does not guarantee outcomes; it governs how professionals conduct themselves when outcomes are uncertain.

Accountability supports longevity. A professional standard must include the ability to review concerns, address misuse of the credential, and protect its integrity. Certification may be suspended or revoked if ethical expectations are violated or if the credential is misrepresented. These safeguards exist to preserve the trust placed in the designation by consumers and institutions alike. Standards endure because they are protected.

The strength of any national framework lies in consistency. Certified professionals across markets operate from shared expectations around communication, restraint, and coordination. This consistency does not replace licensing or regulatory obligations. It complements them. Licensing governs legal authority. Certification reinforces interpretive alignment and professional discipline. Together, they create stability.

Public accountability also benefits professionals. A verifiable credential signals preparation without requiring self-promotion. It allows professionals to demonstrate commitment to structured guidance rather than relying on experience alone. Consumers gain clarity. Institutions gain confidence. Professionals gain differentiation rooted in behavior rather than marketing.

Certification integrity requires independence from commercial influence. A professional standard must be evaluated on its educational merit, not on its ability to drive business activity. For this reason, certification governance remains separate from marketplace participation, referral relationships, or promotional considerations. The standard must serve clarity first. Ultimately, this chapter is not about administration. It is about trust. Renewal ensures currency. Public verification ensures transparency. Ethics commitment ensures behavior aligns with principles. Accountability ensures durability. Together, these elements transform certification from a credential into infrastructure.

Professional standards do not endure because they are announced. They endure because they are maintained. Middle Credit Score® Certification exists to reinforce alignment across roles, protect consumers during complex decisions, and provide institutions with a consistent interpretive framework. Its integrity depends on structure, and that structure is what allows the standard to scale nationally without losing credibility.

That is how certification becomes more than recognition. It becomes a framework that professionals uphold and consumers can rely upon.

Chapter 14:
Certification as a National Standard

Credit plays a central role in real estate outcomes, yet credit literacy has never been a formal part of real estate education. Licensing prepares professionals to understand contracts, disclosures, and fiduciary responsibility, but it does not provide a shared framework for understanding how credit influences timing, affordability, or decision making. As a result, credit often becomes the most important factor in a transaction that no one is formally trained to explain or coordinate around.

This gap is not the result of neglect. It is the result of how education evolved. Real estate and lending developed as separate disciplines, each with its own licensing requirements and continuing education standards. Credit literacy exists between those disciplines, influencing both, yet belonging fully to neither. Middle Credit Score® Certification was created to address that gap without disrupting existing structures. It fits naturally alongside continuing education, brokerage training, and professional development because it complements what already exists rather than attempting to replace it.

Middle Credit Score® Certification is designed to support clarity, not authority. It does not attempt to license professionals or redefine roles. Instead, it provides a shared understanding of how credit affects outcomes and how professionals can operate responsibly within their defined boundaries. This approach allows certification to scale without conflict. It reinforces existing education by adding context and coordination rather than introducing competing standards.

National consistency matters because consumers move, markets change, and expectations travel across state lines. When professionals operate from different assumptions about credit, outcomes become unpredictable. Certification creates a common language that can be applied across markets without overriding local practices or regulatory requirements. That consistency benefits consumers by reducing confusion and benefits professionals by creating alignment across teams and transactions.

For continuing education providers, certification represents alignment rather than disruption. For brokerages, it offers a way to promote professionalism and reduce risk without expanding liability. For institutions and employers, it provides legitimacy as an educational framework that improves understanding without replacing licensed advice. By filling a real and persistent gap, certification improves outcomes across markets and reinforces why it belongs as a national standard within the broader professional ecosystem.

Why Credit Literacy Has Always Lived in the Gaps

Real estate and lending professionals receive extensive training in contracts, compliance, ethics, and process. What has always been missing is a shared framework for understanding how credit actually influences outcomes across roles. Credit touches everything, yet it lives in the gaps between professions.

That gap has never been intentional. It exists because credit sits at the intersection of lending, real estate, consumer behavior, and timing. No single license covers it fully. As a result, education around credit has been assumed rather than taught, and coordination has been left to individual experience rather than shared standards.

A national certification exists to close that gap without rewriting the system.

Why Certification Fits Naturally Into Continuing Education

Certification works best when it complements what already exists. Middle Credit Score® Certification does not replace licensing, continuing education, or professional standards. It fits alongside them by addressing what those systems were never designed to teach.

Continuing education focuses on compliance and competency within a role. Certification focuses on alignment across roles. That distinction allows certification to enhance existing education without conflict. It provides shared language, shared expectations, and shared boundaries that professionals can carry into every transaction.

For CE providers, this alignment matters. Certification adds value without adding friction.

Consistency Matters More Than Customization

Markets differ. Regulations vary. Consumers change. What does not change is the need for consistency in how credit is understood and communicated. A national standard does not eliminate local nuance. It provides a stable foundation professionals can rely on regardless of geography.

Consistency benefits consumers first. When guidance feels predictable and coordinated, trust increases. Professionals benefit as well, because fewer transactions are disrupted by misalignment or misunderstanding. Certification creates this consistency without imposing rigid rules or one-size-fits-all solutions.

Why Brokerages Care About Shared Standards

Brokerages carry responsibility not just for production, but for professionalism and risk. When agents operate

with varying levels of understanding around credit, outcomes become unpredictable. Certification provides brokerages with a way to establish a baseline of clarity without asking agents to become credit experts.
A shared certification standard allows brokerages to reinforce boundaries, reduce liability, and improve coordination with lending partners. It signals professionalism to consumers while supporting agents with education that protects rather than overwhelms.

Why Lenders Benefit From National Alignment

Lenders operate across markets, teams, and timelines. Misalignment creates inefficiency, frustration, and reputational risk. Certification provides a common reference point that improves communication with Realtors and consumers alike.

When lenders align with a national standard, they are not claiming superiority. They are signaling consistency. That signal reduces friction and builds trust with referral partners, institutions, and the consumers they serve.

Why Employers and Institutions Pay Attention

Employers, HR teams, and unions increasingly recognize that financial literacy impacts employee stability and well-being. Housing decisions are among the most consequential financial moments in an employee's life. Confusion during those moments carries real costs.

A certification framework focused on clarity and consumer protection fits naturally into employer education initiatives. It offers a neutral, non-promotional way to support informed decision-making without crossing into advice or product endorsement. Institutions care because clarity scales better than intervention.

Certification Scales Without Conflict

One of the strongest arguments for a national standard is its ability to scale cleanly. Middle Credit Score® Certification does not compete with existing education. It does not require regulatory change. It does not create exclusivity or hierarchy.

It scales because it focuses on alignment, not authority. It improves outcomes by reducing confusion, not by promising results. That scalability is what allows certification to function as infrastructure rather than a temporary solution.

What This Chapter Is Really Saying

This chapter is not about credentialing. It is about legitimacy. A national standard exists because the system needs shared understanding more than it needs more rules. Certification fills a real gap by creating consistency across roles without disrupting existing structures.

When education aligns professionals rather than separating them, outcomes improve quietly and reliably. That is how standards endure. Not through force, but through usefulness.

Chapter 15:
How Consumers Should Choose Professionals

Choosing the right professionals is one of the most important decisions a consumer makes in a real estate or lending process, yet most consumers are never taught how to make that choice with confidence. They often rely on familiarity, personality, or reassurance, assuming that experience alone guarantees alignment. While those qualities can matter, they do not explain how a professional approaches credit, communicates under pressure, or respects boundaries when outcomes are at stake.

Certification simplifies this decision by shifting the focus from impressions to signals. A certified professional does not need to prove competence through charisma or marketing. Their approach becomes evident in how they explain the process, how they set expectations, and how they respond when uncertainty appears. Consumers begin to notice whether a professional prioritizes clarity over urgency, education over opinion, and coordination over assumption. These signals matter more than years in business alone because they reveal how guidance will be delivered when it matters most.

Advocating for oneself does not require confrontation. Consumers can ask thoughtful, neutral questions and listen for how those questions are answered. A professional who welcomes clarity, respects boundaries, and explains roles without defensiveness is demonstrating alignment. A professional who relies on reassurance without explanation or discourages coordination is revealing a different approach. Certification makes these differences easier to recognize without placing the consumer in an adversarial position.

Middle Credit Score® Certification helps consumers move from uncertainty to confidence by offering a simple way to evaluate guidance before consequences appear. When consumers understand what certification signals, they spend less time guessing and more time choosing professionals who align with their needs. Over time, certified professionals stand out naturally, not because they demand attention, but because their approach creates trust. That trust changes outcomes and explains why certification matters long before a transaction begins.

Most Consumers Choose Based on What They Can See

Consumers usually choose professionals based on the information that is easiest to access. A referral from someone they trust. A website that feels polished. A conversation that sounds confident. None of these are wrong, but none of them explain how a professional will operate once the process becomes complex.

Confidence is visible. Alignment is not. That is why consumers often assume competence based on tone rather than structure. Certification exists to make the invisible visible, so consumers can choose based on how professionals work, not just how they present themselves.

Why the Right Questions Matter More Than the Right Answers

Consumers are often focused on answers. Rates. Timelines. Approval likelihood. These questions are understandable, but they do not reveal how a professional handles uncertainty, boundaries, or coordination.

The most important questions are often structural rather than transactional. How does this professional explain credit without overstepping? How do they coordinate with others in the process? What happens when information changes? Certification signals that these questions have already been addressed through education, not improvisation.

Signals to Look for Before You Commit

Consumers do not need to interrogate professionals or challenge their expertise. They can look for signals instead. Does the professional explain what they do and what they do not do? Do they redirect certain questions

rather than answering everything themselves? Do they
emphasize coordination over control?

These signals suggest discipline and alignment. Certified
professionals tend to speak calmly about process, timing,
and roles. They are less likely to make sweeping
assurances and more likely to frame decisions in context.
These behaviors indicate preparation rather than
persuasion.

Why Certification Simplifies the Decision

Certification reduces the burden on consumers. Instead
of comparing personalities, promises, or marketing
claims, consumers can focus on alignment. Certification
does not tell consumers who to choose. It tells them how
a professional approaches their role.

This distinction matters. Consumers are not selecting
outcomes. They are selecting guidance. When guidance is
structured and consistent, outcomes become more
predictable. Certification provides a shortcut to
confidence without eliminating choice.

How to Advocate for Yourself Without Creating Tension

Self-advocacy does not require confrontation. Consumers
can ask clarifying questions and request coordination

without challenging authority. Asking how professionals work together or when certain conversations should happen invites alignment rather than resistance. Certified professionals are receptive to these questions because they are trained to operate within clear boundaries. They understand that informed consumers are not obstacles. They are partners in a more stable process.

Why Charisma and Experience Alone Are Not Enough

Experience matters, so does communication skill however, what neither guarantees is consistency. Two professionals with similar backgrounds can operate very differently under pressure. Certification addresses this gap by establishing shared expectations that experience alone does not provide.

Consumers benefit because certification reduces variability. It does not promise perfection. It promises structure. That structure becomes especially valuable when conditions change and decisions become more nuanced.

Choosing Professionals Is Really Choosing a Process

When consumers choose professionals, they are choosing a process, whether they realize it or not. They are choosing how information will flow, how decisions will be framed, and how surprises will be handled.

Certified professionals offer a process grounded in alignment, restraint, and clarity. Consumers who choose them are not choosing faster or easier paths. They are choosing steadier ones.

What This Chapter Is Really Saying

This chapter is not about teaching consumers to judge professionals. It is about helping them recognize alignment when they see it. Certification makes that recognition easier by signaling how professionals operate before pressure arrives.

When consumers choose aligned professionals, they reduce the need to guess. They move from hope to understanding. That shift alone changes outcomes more than most people realize.

Chapter 16:
The Future of Aligned Lending and Real Estate

The real estate and lending process continues to move faster. Decisions are made more quickly, systems rely more heavily on automation, and explanations are often shortened or removed entirely. What once unfolded through a series of conversations now moves through digital steps that prioritize speed and efficiency. While these changes can increase access and convenience, they also reduce opportunities for clarity. As complexity increases, alignment becomes more important, not less.

Consumers feel this shift even when they cannot name it. They encounter decisions that carry long term consequences without fully understanding how those decisions are evaluated. As a result, they begin to value guidance that explains rather than reassures. They seek professionals who slow the right moments, set expectations early, and respect the limits of their role. Over time, consumers gravitate toward education because it creates confidence that speed alone cannot provide.

In this environment, professionals are not differentiated by volume, marketing, or momentum. They are differentiated by how they guide consumers through complexity. Those who can explain what matters, coordinate effectively, and exercise restraint when appropriate become trusted over the long term. Education scales better than advice because it empowers consumers without requiring constant intervention. Alignment scales because it creates consistency across teams, markets, and transactions.

Middle Credit Score® Certification exists to support this future. It is not a response to a trend or a tactic designed to capture attention. It is a framework built to endure as systems evolve. By emphasizing education, role clarity, and ethical boundaries, certification prepares professionals to adapt without losing trust. It provides consumers with a way to recognize alignment even as processes become more automated and less explained.

Looking forward, alignment becomes the anchor that holds outcomes together. Certified professionals are prepared, adaptable, and trusted because they understand that guidance matters most when systems move quickly. As lending and real estate continue to change, certification remains steady. It offers clarity in complexity and reassurance without urgency. That is why alignment leads, and why certification matters long term.

The Process Is Moving Faster, Even When Understanding Is Not

Lending and real estate are accelerating. Automation is increasing. Decisions are happening more quickly. Systems are designed to reduce friction and compress timelines. On the surface, this feels like progress.

At the same time, explanations are getting thinner. Consumers are expected to move quickly with less context. Professionals are expected to produce outcomes in environments where complexity has not disappeared, it has simply been hidden behind technology.

Speed has improved. Understanding has not always kept pace.

This imbalance is where alignment becomes essential.

As Systems Accelerate, Coordination Matters More

When processes slow down, misalignment can sometimes be corrected quietly. When processes speed up, misalignment becomes visible immediately. Confusion shows up faster. Mixed messages collide sooner. Small misunderstandings carry greater consequences.

The future of lending and real estate will not be defined by who moves the fastest. It will be defined by who can coordinate clearly under pressure. Alignment becomes the stabilizing force when systems move faster than human understanding.

Certified professionals are prepared for this environment because their guidance does not rely on improvisation.

Education Scales Better Than Advice

Advice is situational. It depends on timing, context, and conditions. Education creates a framework that can adapt as conditions change. This distinction matters more as processes evolve.

The future favors professionals who can help consumers interpret information rather than react to it. Consumers will continue to seek guidance, but they will increasingly value those who explain why things happen, not just what to do next.

Certification supports this shift by grounding professionals in shared understanding rather than isolated tactics.

Consumers Will Demand Clarity, Not Reassurance

As access to information increases, consumers are becoming more aware of how little is explained during critical decisions. They are asking better questions. They are noticing inconsistencies. They are less satisfied with reassurance that is not supported by clarity.

The professionals who thrive in the future will not be the loudest or most confident voices. They will be the ones who can calmly explain complexity without overwhelming the consumer. Alignment allows that explanation to remain consistent across roles and moments of stress.

Differentiation Will Come From How Professionals Guide, Not What They Offer

Products change. Programs evolve. Market conditions shift. What remains constant is how professionals guide consumers through uncertainty. That guidance is what consumers remember.

The future will differentiate professionals based on behavior, not volume. On restraint, not promises. On coordination, not control. Certification supports this differentiation by setting expectations around how professionals operate rather than what they sell.

Why Alignment Is Not a Trend

Trends come and go. Alignment endures because it solves a structural problem. It reduces confusion, preserves trust, and stabilizes outcomes across changing environments.

Middle Credit Score® Certification is not tied to a specific market cycle or technology. It is tied to how humans process information during complex decisions. As long as lending and real estate involve pressure, emotion, and consequence, alignment will matter.

Prepared Professionals Will Be Trusted Long-Term

Consumers do not remember every detail of a transaction. They remember how it felt. Whether it felt chaotic or controlled. Whether they felt informed or rushed. Whether they trusted the people guiding them.

Professionals who operate with alignment create experiences that feel steady even when outcomes are uncertain. That steadiness builds trust that lasts beyond a single transaction.

The future rewards professionals who are prepared, adaptable, and grounded in shared understanding.

What This Chapter Is Really Saying

This chapter is not about what is coming next. It is about what will always matter. As systems change, alignment remains the constant that protects consumers and professionals alike.

Certification is not future proof because it predicts the future. It is future-proof because it prepares professionals to operate with clarity no matter how the environment evolves.

Why Certification Matters

Certification matters because complexity has increased, while shared understanding has not always kept pace.

Real estate and lending continue to evolve. Processes accelerate. Technology compresses timelines. Expectations rise. Yet the human experience of navigating credit-driven decisions remains vulnerable to confusion when roles are unclear and communication is inconsistent. Speed has improved. Access has expanded. But interpretation still requires discipline.

Most breakdowns in transactions do not occur because professionals lack effort or intent. They occur because alignment was never formally reinforced. When guidance overlaps, when messages conflict, or when decisions are made without shared context, consumers absorb the consequences. The cost may appear as delay, frustration, uncertainty, or credit disruption, but its root is often structural rather than personal.

Certification exists to reduce that variability.

For consumers, certification provides observable signals. It removes the need to guess whether guidance is coordinated. It replaces blind trust with structured clarity. It does not promise outcomes. It reinforces behavior. When professionals operate from shared expectations, the process becomes steadier even when circumstances are not.

CONCLUSION

For professionals, certification establishes a common framework that strengthens communication and reduces friction across roles. It emphasizes restraint, sequencing, and boundary awareness rather than momentum alone. It allows experience to operate within structure. That structure reduces mixed messages and supports decisions grounded in context rather than assumption.

For institutions, certification functions as infrastructure. It complements licensing, continuing education, and compliance systems without competing with them. It improves consistency without introducing regulatory conflict. Its value lies not in exclusivity, but in predictability. Standards endure when they align with existing systems rather than attempt to replace them.

What makes certification matter is not the credential itself. It is the discipline it reinforces. Asking questions earlier. Pausing when necessary. Coordinating before assumptions solidify. Protecting credit through restraint rather than urgency. These behaviors rarely attract attention, but they prevent harm.

Clarity is rarely dramatic. It works quietly. Consumers may not always recognize what was avoided: the unnecessary inquiry, the delayed conversation, the conflicting advice that never surfaced. Protection is often invisible when it functions properly. Its presence is felt through steadiness rather than spectacle.

Annual renewal, public verification, and ethical commitment reinforce durability. Without maintenance, credentials weaken. With structure, they scale. Renewal confirms continued alignment. Public verification strengthens transparency. Ethical accountability preserves trust. These elements transform certification from recognition into governance.

As systems continue to evolve, automation will increase and timelines will compress further. What will not change is the need for coordinated human judgment. Alignment cannot be automated. Role clarity cannot be improvised under pressure. Standards provide continuity in environments that otherwise move quickly.

Middle Credit Score® Certification was built to function as a durable framework — one that supports consumers, professionals, and institutions equally. It does not promise certainty. It reinforces consistency. It does not eliminate complexity. It organizes it.

Standards are not built for a single transaction. They are built to endure across markets, cycles, and generations of professionals. Certification matters not because it is new, but because it addresses a structural gap that has existed for decades.

Not as a marketing tool.

Not as a shortcut.

But as a standard for how complex decisions should be guided.

That is why certification matters.

Middle Credit Score® Certified Professional Ethics and Professional Commitment

As a Middle Credit Score® Certified Professional, I affirm the following commitments:

1. **Role Clarity**
   I will operate strictly within the scope of my licensed authority and professional responsibility. I will not provide credit interpretation, financial advice, or guidance beyond my defined role.

2. **Consumer Protection First**
   I will prioritize clarity, transparency, and long-term consumer stability over transactional urgency or short-term momentum.

3. **Coordination Over Assumption**
   I will promote alignment by coordinating appropriately with other licensed professionals involved in the transaction and avoiding overlapping or conflicting guidance.

4. **Restraint When Necessary**
   I will recognize when pausing, redirecting, or sequencing conversations protects the consumer more effectively than immediate action.

5. **Credit Preservation Awareness**
   I will avoid encouraging unnecessary credit activity or actions that may create unintended harm during active lending or real estate processes.

6. **Integrity in Representation**
   I will represent my certification accurately and will not imply guarantees, endorsements, or outcomes that certification does not provide.

7. **Ongoing Renewal Commitment**
   I acknowledge that certification requires annual renewal and continued adherence to these principles.

Failure to uphold these commitments may result in review, suspension, or revocation of certification status. This certification reflects adherence to a professional alignment standard. It does not constitute legal, financial, or underwriting authority.

Glenn Clark is a real estate broker, former top-producing loan officer, and the founder of Middle Credit Score®. He has spent more than three decades working across the mortgage and real estate industries, guiding consumers through complex financial decisions at moments when clarity matters most.

Glenn is a graduate of ASU's W. P. Carey School of Business, where his formal business education reinforced what decades of real-world experience had already taught him: outcomes improve when systems are designed around understanding, not assumption.

Over the course of his career, Glenn has worked directly with thousands of consumers, from first-time buyers to experienced homeowners, and has held roles as a top-producing loan officer, sales leader, mortgage company owner, and now real estate broker. That perspective—having operated on both sides of the transaction—shapes his focus on alignment, role clarity, and consumer protection.

Glenn created Middle Credit Score® to address a recurring problem he observed throughout his career: consumers were being asked to make high-stakes decisions without a clear framework for understanding how credit is evaluated or how professionals should coordinate when challenges arise. Rather than offering tactics or promises, his work emphasizes education, restraint, and shared understanding as the foundation for better outcomes.

ABOUT THE AUTHOR

He is particularly passionate about helping consumers navigate moments of uncertainty without pressure or confusion, and about supporting lenders and Realtors who want to operate with professionalism, consistency, and long-term trust. His work with certification, continuing education, and professional alignment is designed to elevate standards without disrupting existing systems.

Glenn lives with his wife, their two daughters, and their dog. When he is not working on consumer education or professional standards, he remains deeply committed to building tools and frameworks that make complex financial decisions easier to understand and less intimidating for the people facing them.

---

www.ingramcontent.com/pod-product-compliance
Lightning Source LLC
Chambersburg PA
CBHW070944210326
41520CB00021B/7039